TUNED IN

A Comprehensive Approach to Band Intonation

BRIAN BALMAGES AND ROBERT HERRINGS

Table of Contents

About This Book:

It is recommended that percussionists focus on marimba and vibraphone (multiple players can be on each instrument in different octaves) with soft mallets. Xylophone (with very soft yarn mallets) may also be used, but the authors suggest avoiding bells altogether as they will be too distracting. All notes in this book should be rolled for their full duration, although no formal roll markings are used in the music.

It is important to observe all phrase markings (slurs), and be sure to physically breathe when the winds do so that you further develop an awareness of when to begin and release each note or phrase. Also focus on smooth changes between notes. Finally, use this as a time to be highly sensitive to the balance between winds and percussion.

A speaker icon is included on lines that have a downloadable drone option, or musicians can use their own device to create a drone.

To access the free downloadable drones, visit **www.fjhmusic.com/downloads** and enter the following authentication code.

Website: www.fjhmusic.com/downloads
Authentication Code: 22283444142

2

CONCERT B♭ MAJOR / G MINOR

1. Chromatic Intervals

Play in any combination. A suggested progression is:
- *Line A alone with recorded drone.* • *Line B alone with recorded drone.*
- *Line A and B combined with drone.* • *A, B and C combined (with and without recorded drone).*

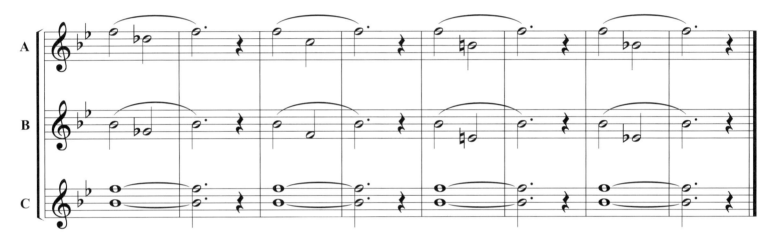

2. Interval Tuning

Play with recorded drone, then without.

3. Isolating Concert B♭

Play with recorded drone, then without.

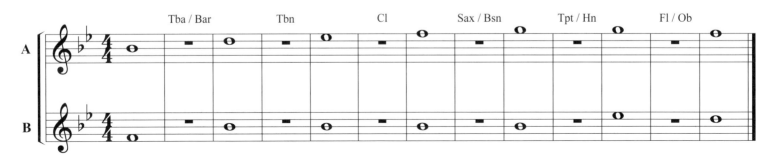

BB212PER

4. Chorale

Play using the following combinations:
- *With recorded drone.*
- *Without recorded drone, having various band members droning on concert B♭ and F.*
- *Chorale alone (without any drone).*

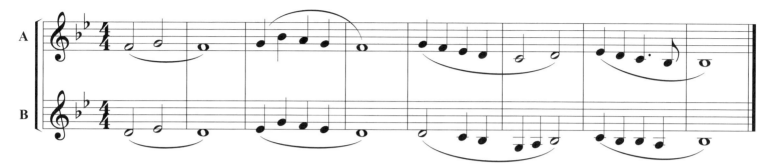

5. Concert G Minor Drone

Play with recorded drone, then without.

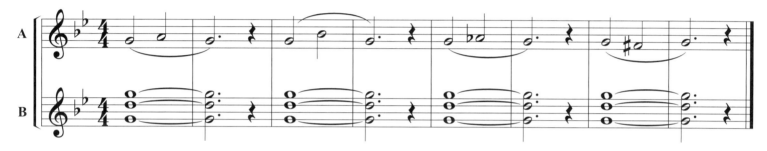

6. Descending Triads

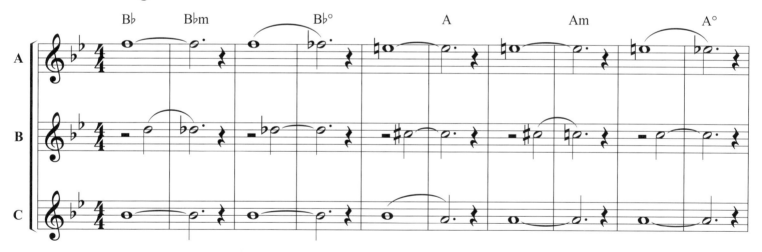

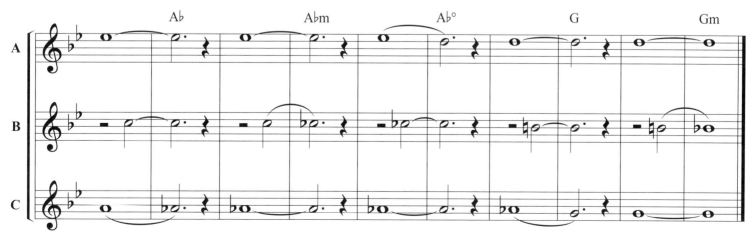

BB212PER

CONCERT E♭ MAJOR / C MINOR

1. Chromatic Intervals

Play in any combination. A suggested progression is:
- *Line A alone with recorded drone.* • *Line B alone with recorded drone.*
- *Line A and B combined with drone.* • *A, B and C combined (with and without recorded drone).*

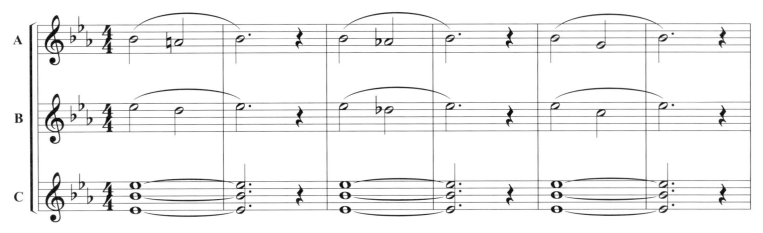

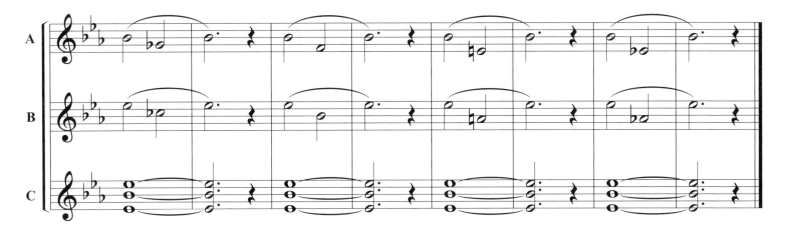

2. Interval Tuning

Play with recorded drone, then without.

3. Isolating Concert E♭

Play with recorded drone, then without.

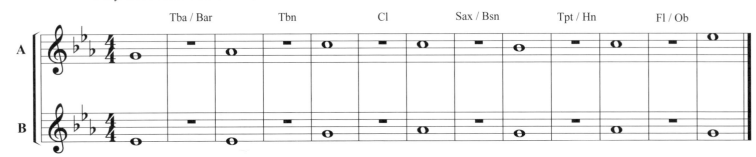

4. Chorale

Play using the following combinations:
- *With recorded drone.*
- *Without recorded drone, having various band members droning on concert E♭.*
- *Chorale alone (without any drone).*

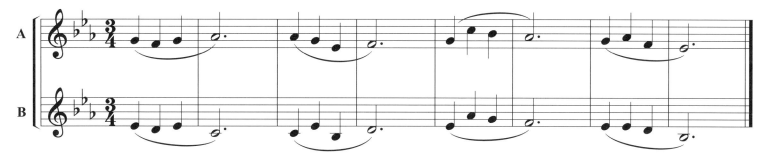

5. Concert C Minor Drone

Play with recorded drone, then without.

6. Descending Triads

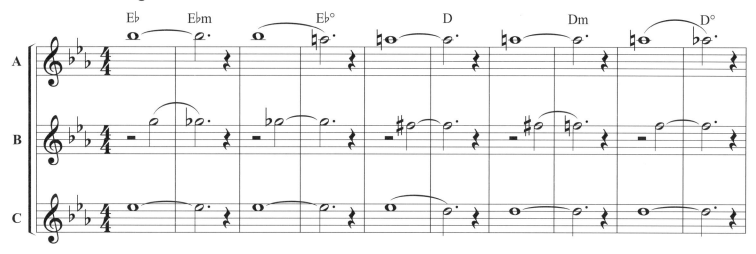

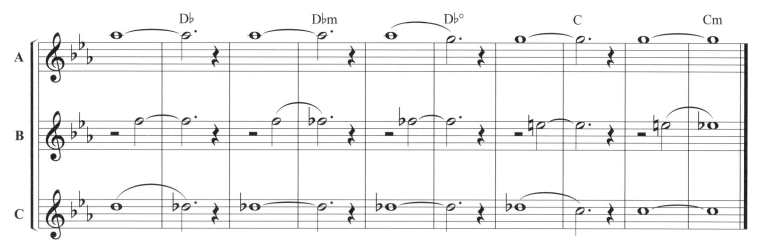

CONCERT F MAJOR / D MINOR

1. Chromatic Intervals

Play in any combination. A suggested progression is:
• Line A alone with recorded drone. • Line B alone with recorded drone.
• Line A and B combined with drone. • A, B and C combined (with and without recorded drone).

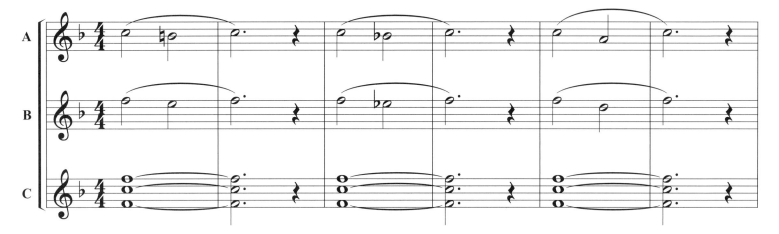

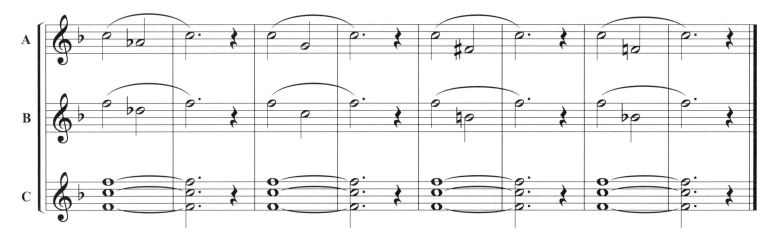

2. Interval Tuning

Play with recorded drone, then without.

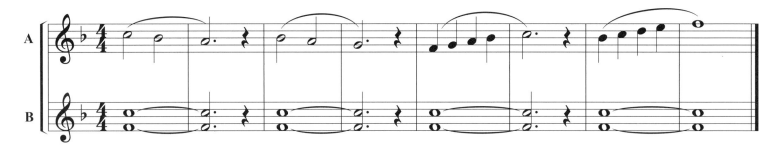

3. Isolating Concert F

Play with recorded drone, then without.

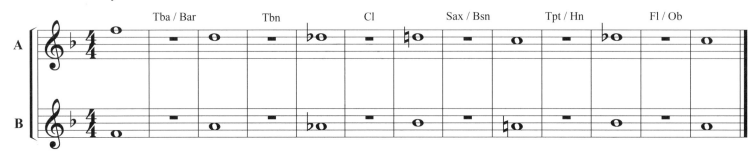

4. Chorale

Play using the following combinations:
- *With recorded drone.*
- *Without recorded drone, having various band members droning on concert F.*
  To further develop aural skills, add a concert C to the drone.
- *Chorale alone (without any drone).*

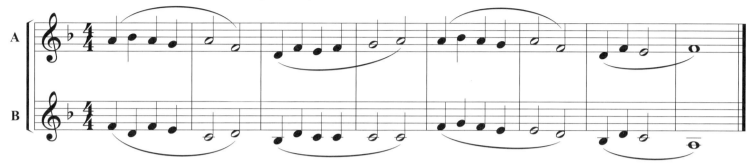

5. Concert D Minor Drone

Play with recorded drone, then without.

6. Descending Triads

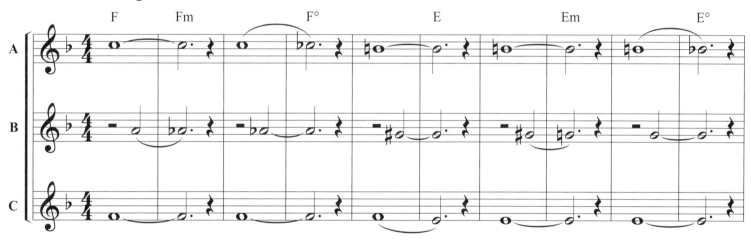

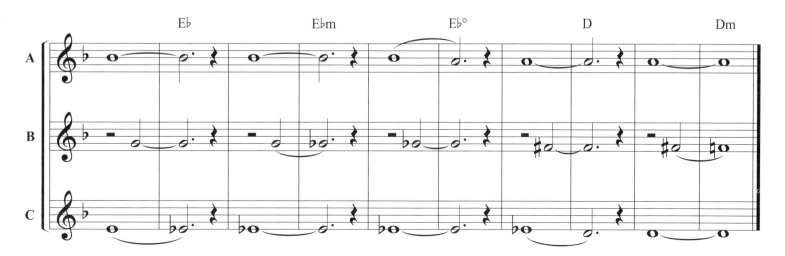

BB212PER

CONCERT C MAJOR / A MINOR

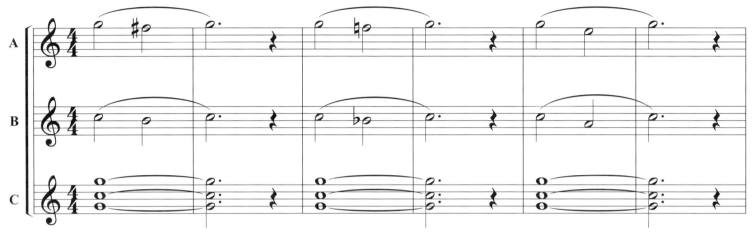

1. Chromatic Intervals
Play in any combination. A suggested progression is:
• Line A alone with recorded drone. • Line B alone with recorded drone.
• Line A and B combined with drone. • A, B and C combined (with and without recorded drone).

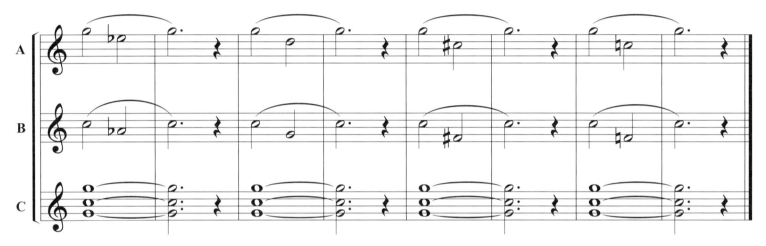

2. Interval Tuning
Play with recorded drone, then without.

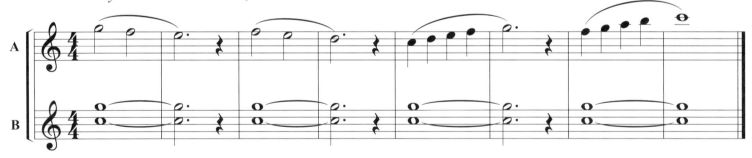

3. Isolating Concert C
Play with recorded drone, then without.

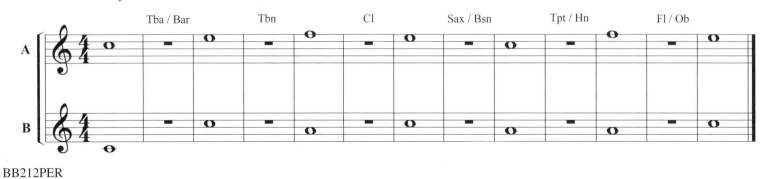

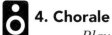

4. Chorale

Play using the following combinations:
- *With recorded drone.*
- *Without recorded drone, having various band members droning on concert C and G.*
- *Chorale alone (without any drone).*

5. Concert A Minor Drone

Play with recorded drone, then without.

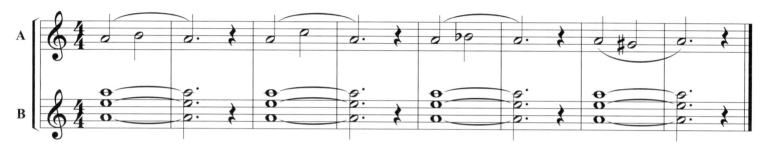

6. Descending Triads

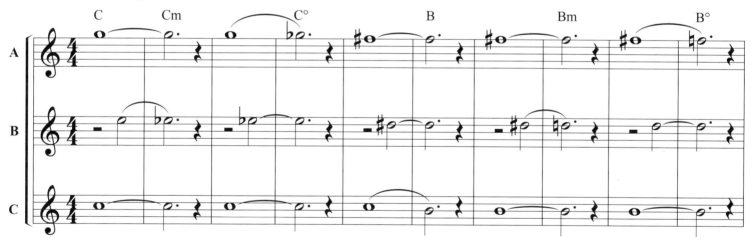

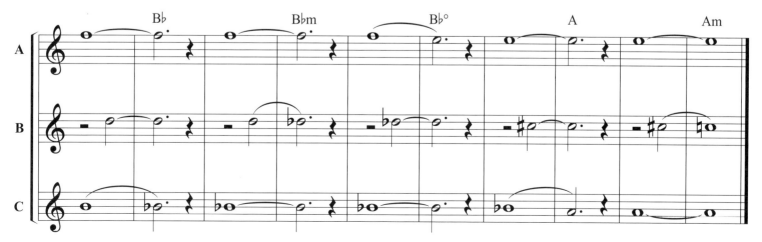

CONCERT G MAJOR / E MINOR

1. Chromatic Intervals

Play in any combination. A suggested progression is:
- *Line A alone with recorded drone.* • *Line B alone with recorded drone.*
- *Line A and B combined with drone.* • *A, B and C combined (with and without recorded drone).*

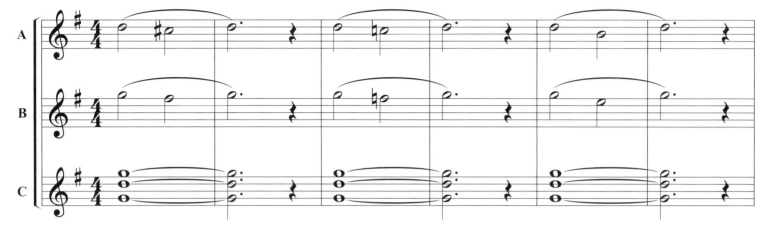

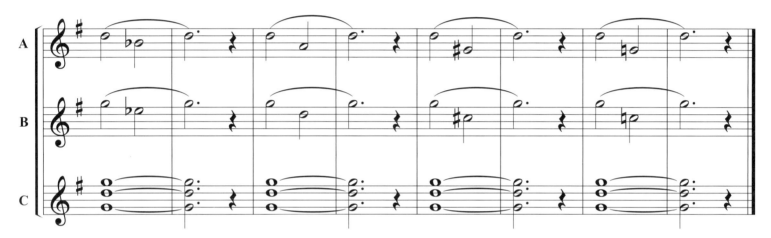

2. Interval Tuning

Play with recorded drone, then without.

3. Isolating Concert G

Play with recorded drone, then without.

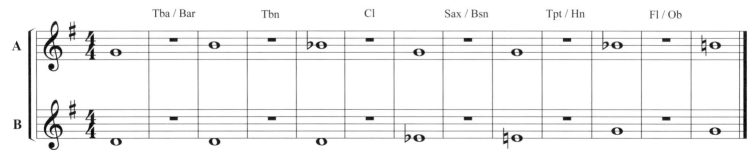

4. Chorale

Play using the following combinations:
- *With recorded drone.*
- *Without recorded drone, having various band members droning on concert G.*
  To further develop aural skills, add a concert D to the drone.
- *Chorale alone (without any drone).*

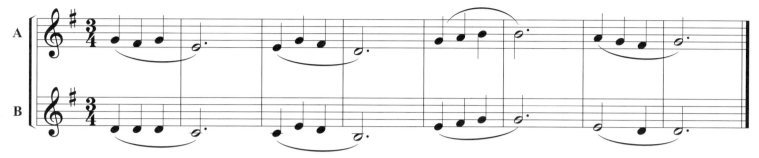

5. Concert E Minor Drone

Play with recorded drone, then without.

6. Descending Triads

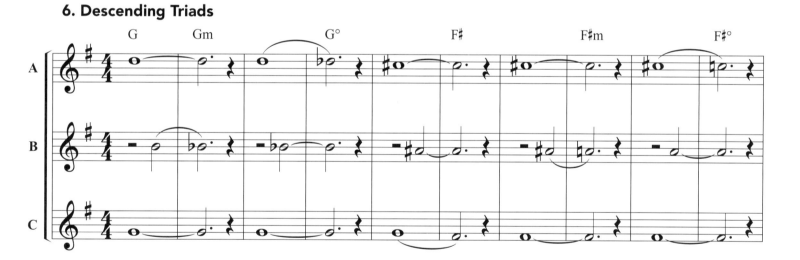

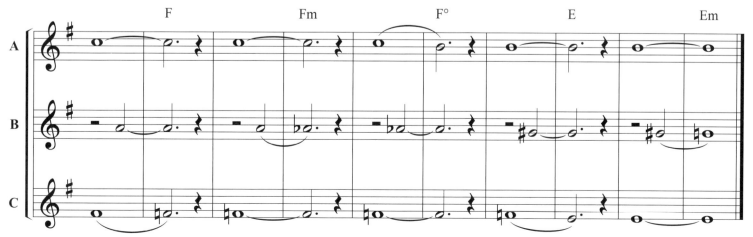

CONCERT D MAJOR / B MINOR

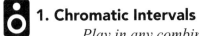

1. Chromatic Intervals

Play in any combination. A suggested progression is:
- *Line A alone with recorded drone.* • *Line B alone with recorded drone.*
- *Line A and B combined with drone.* • *A, B and C combined (with and without recorded drone).*

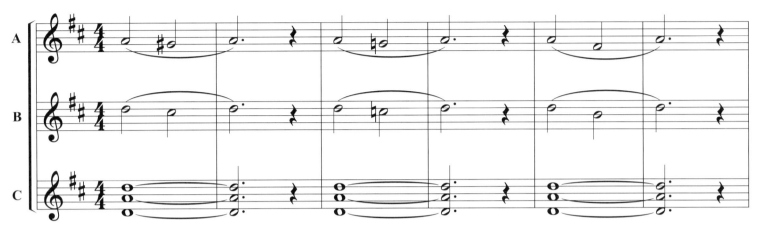

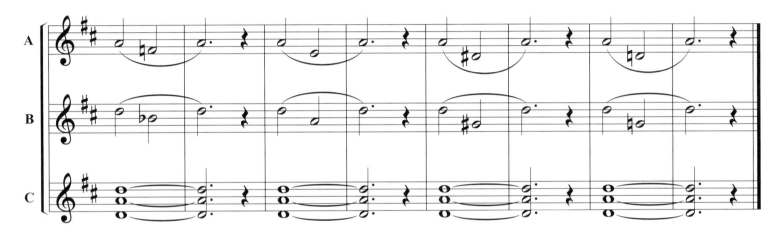

2. Interval Tuning

Play with recorded drone, then without.

3. Isolating Concert D

Play with recorded drone, then without.

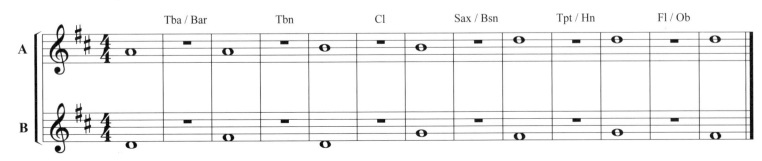

4. Chorale

In addition to playing the chorale alone, using a drone on concert D (recorded or played) will really stretch the ear in measure 4.

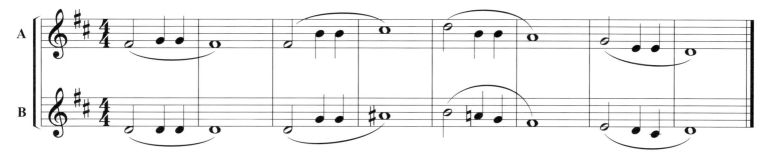

5. Concert B Minor Drone

Play with recorded drone, then without.

6. Descending Triads

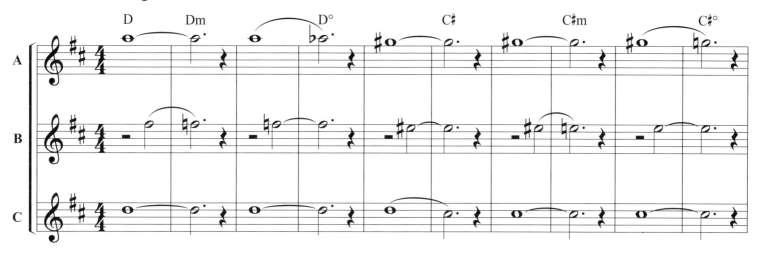

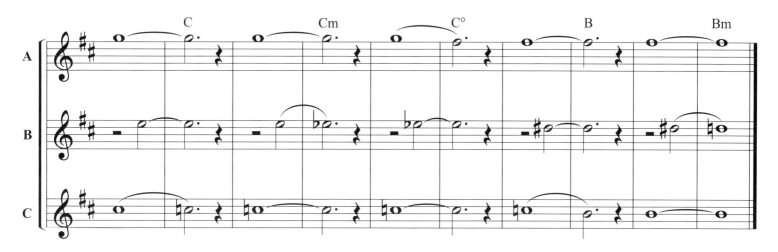

14

CONCERT A MAJOR / F# MINOR

1. Chromatic Intervals

Play in any combination. A suggested progression is:
- *Line A alone with recorded drone.* • *Line B alone with recorded drone.*
- *Line A and B combined with drone.* • *A, B and C combined (with and without recorded drone).*

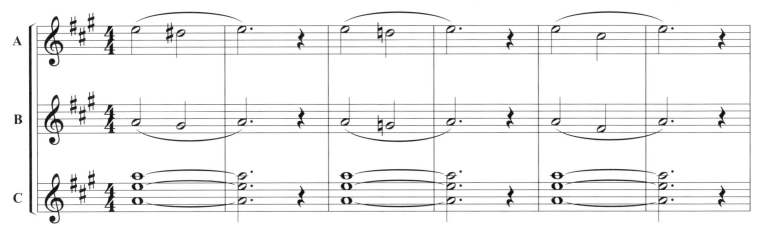

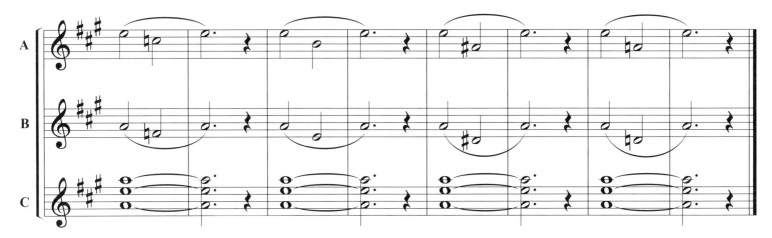

2. Interval Tuning

Play with recorded drone, then without.

3. Isolating Concert A

Play with recorded drone, then without.

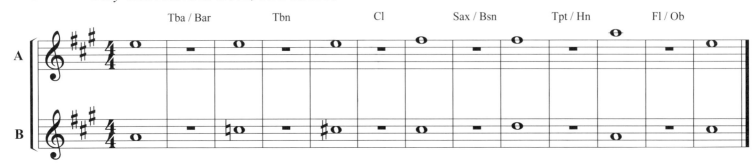

BB212PER

4. Chorale

Play using the following combinations:
- *With recorded drone.*
- *Without recorded drone, having various band members droning on concert A.*
  To further develop aural skills, add a concert E to the drone.
- *Chorale alone (without any drone).*

5. Concert F♯ Minor Drone

Play with recorded drone, then without.

6. Descending Triads

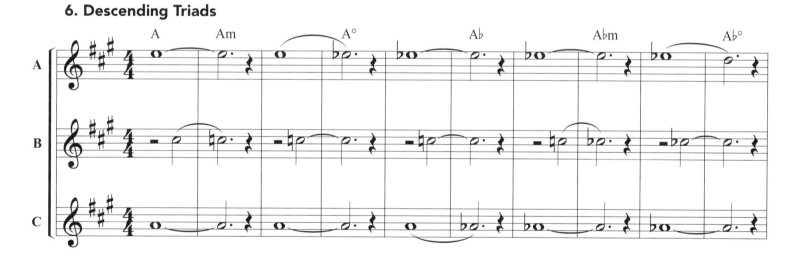

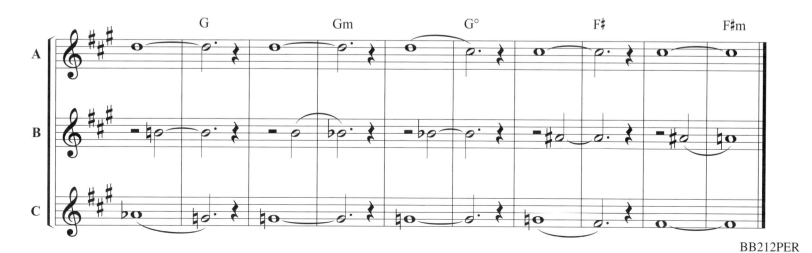

CONCERT E MAJOR / C♯ MINOR

1. Chromatic Intervals

Play in any combination. A suggested progression is:
• Line A alone with recorded drone. • Line B alone with recorded drone.
• Line A and B combined with drone. • A, B and C combined (with and without recorded drone).

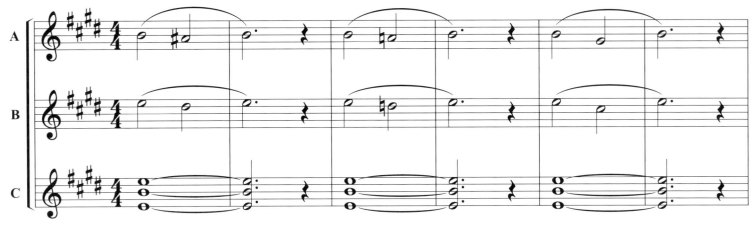

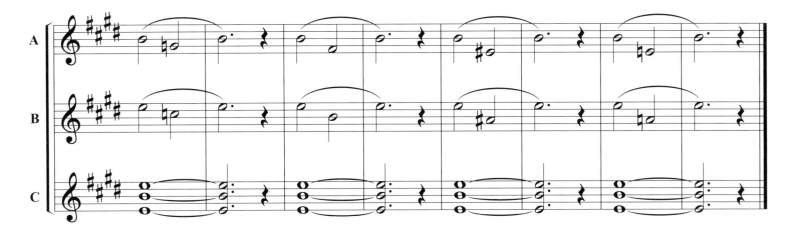

2. Interval Tuning

Play with recorded drone, then without.

3. Isolating Concert E

Play with recorded drone, then without.

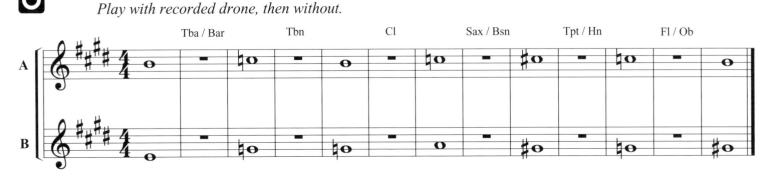

4. Chorale

Play using the following combinations:
- *With recorded drone.*
- *Without recorded drone, having various band members droning on concert E.*
- *Chorale alone (without any drone).*

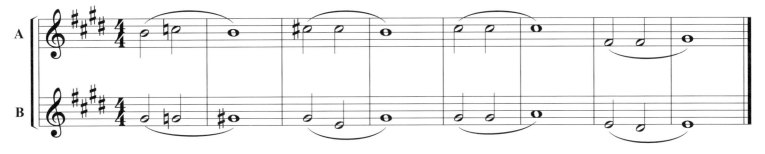

5. Concert C♯ Minor Drone

Play with recorded drone, then without.

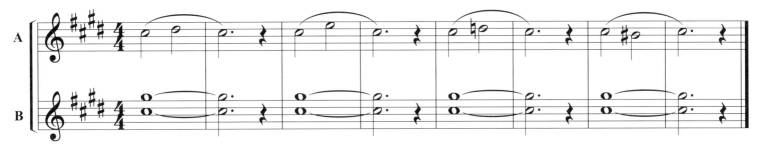

6. Descending Triads

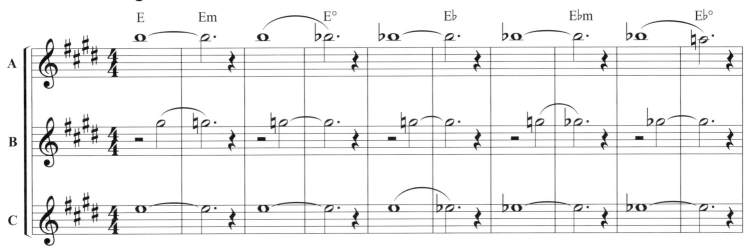

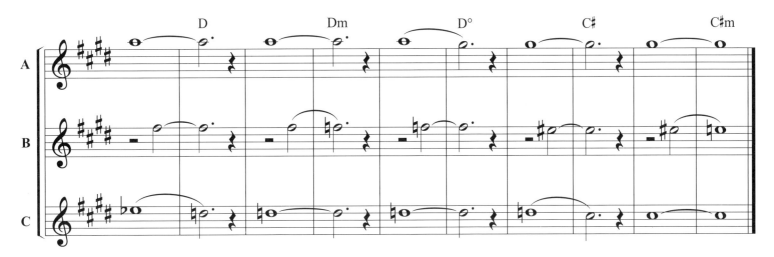

CONCERT B MAJOR / G♯ MINOR

 1. Chromatic Intervals

Play in any combination. A suggested progression is:
- *Line A alone with recorded drone.* • *Line B alone with recorded drone.*
- *Line A and B combined with drone.* • *A, B and C combined (with and without recorded drone).*

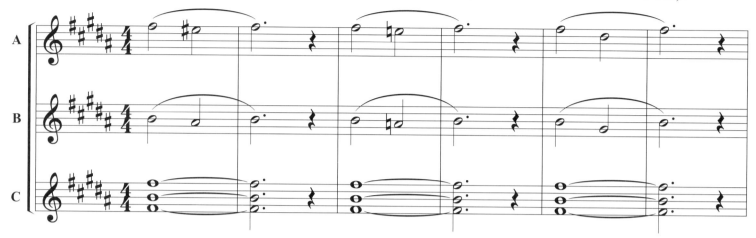

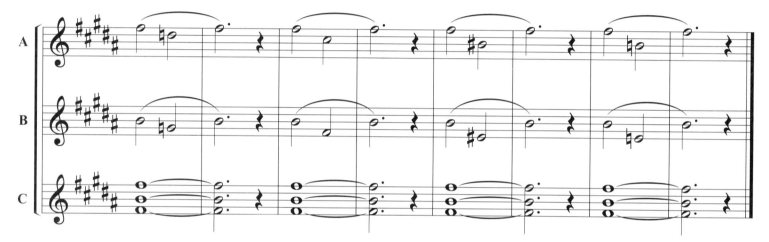

 2. Interval Tuning

Play with recorded drone, then without.

 3. Isolating Concert B

Play with recorded drone, then without.

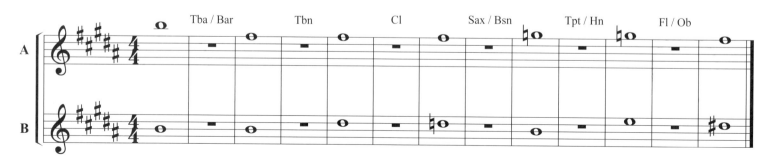

4. Chorale

Play using the following combinations:
- *With recorded drone.*
- *Without recorded drone, having various band members droning on concert B.*
  To further develop aural skills, add a concert F♯ to the drone.
- *Chorale alone (without any drone).*

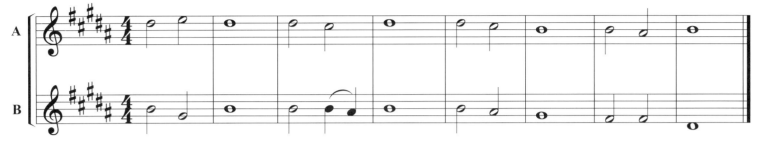

5. Concert G♯ Minor Drone

Play with recorded drone, then without.

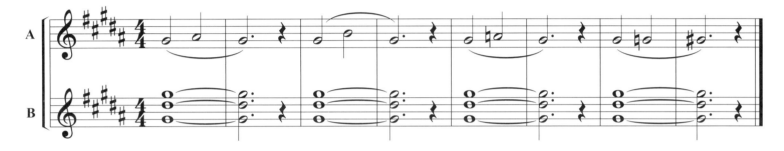

6. Descending Triads

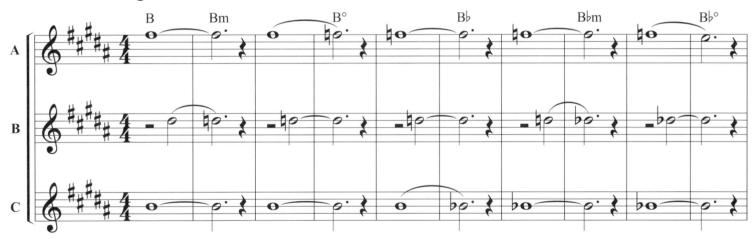

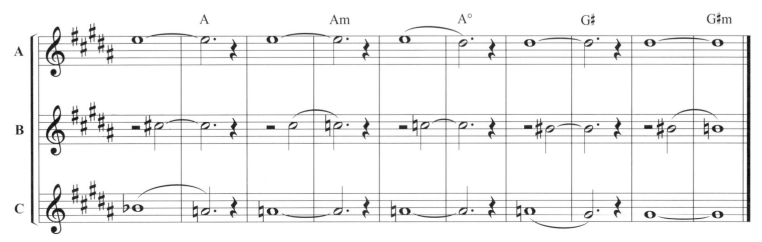

BB212PER

CONCERT G♭ MAJOR / E♭ MINOR

1. Chromatic Intervals

Play in any combination. A suggested progression is:
- *Line A alone with recorded drone.* • *Line B alone with recorded drone.*
- *Line A and B combined with drone.* • *A, B and C combined (with and without recorded drone).*

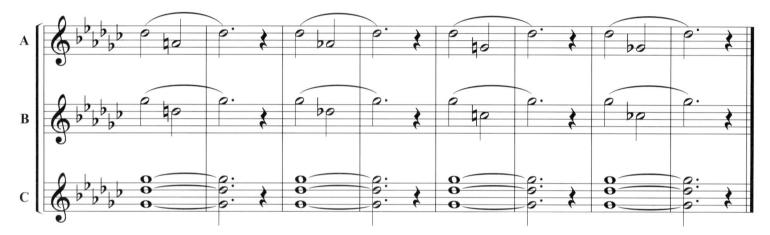

2. Interval Tuning

Play with recorded drone, then without.

3. Isolating Concert G♭

Play with recorded drone, then without.

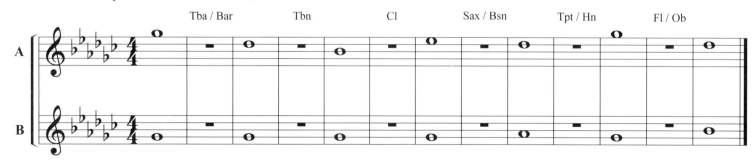

4. Chorale

Play using the following combinations:
- *With recorded drone.*
- *Without recorded drone, having various band members droning on concert Gb.*
   To further develop aural skills, add a concert Db to the drone.
- *Chorale alone (without any drone).*

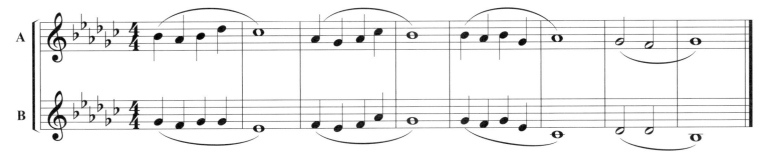

5. Concert Eb Minor Drone

Play with recorded drone, then without.

6. Descending Triads

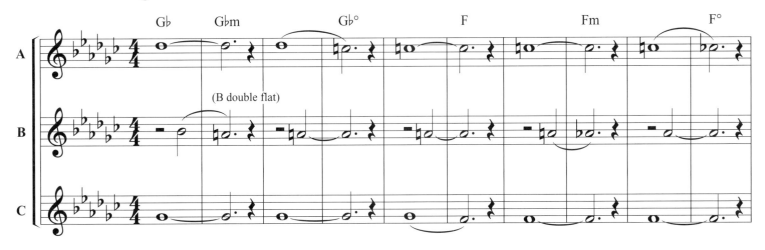

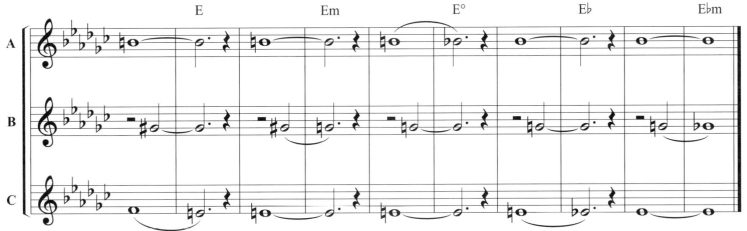

BB212PER

CONCERT D♭ MAJOR / B♭ MINOR

1. Chromatic Intervals

Play in any combination. A suggested progression is:
- *Line A alone with recorded drone.* • *Line B alone with recorded drone.*
- *Line A and B combined with drone.* • *A, B and C combined (with and without recorded drone).*

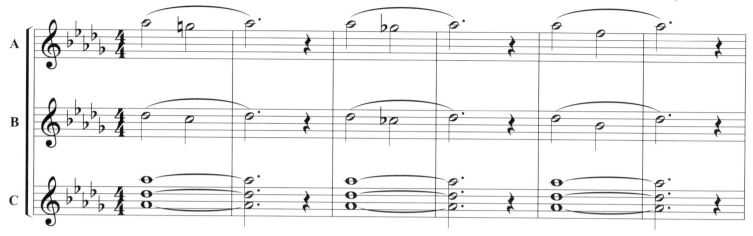

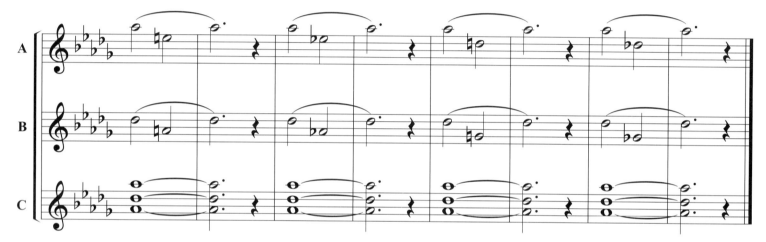

2. Interval Tuning

Play with recorded drone, then without.

3. Isolating Concert D♭

Play with recorded drone, then without.

Tba / Bar   Tbn   Cl   Sax / Bsn   Tpt / Hn   Fl / Ob

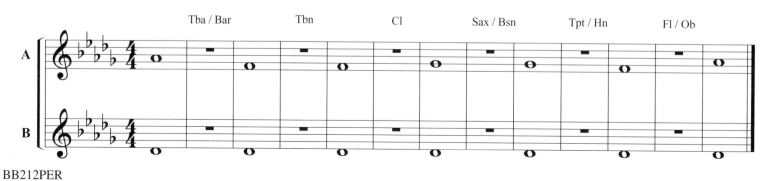

BB212PER

4. Chorale

Play using the following combinations:
- *With recorded drone.*
- *Without recorded drone, having various band members droning on concert Db.*
  To further develop aural skills, add a concert Ab to the drone.
- *Chorale alone (without any drone).*

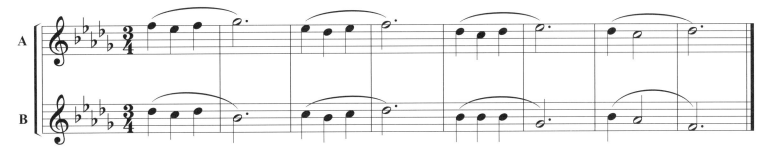

5. Concert Bb Minor Drone

Play with recorded drone, then without.

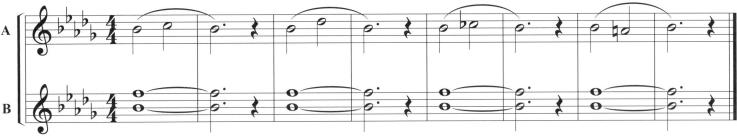

6. Descending Triads

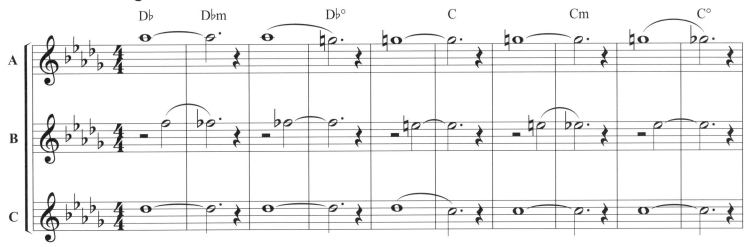

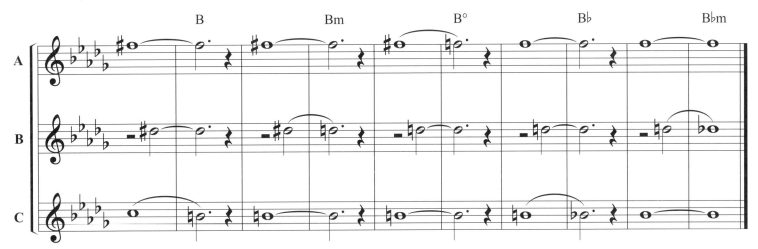

BB212PER

24

CONCERT A♭ MAJOR / F MINOR

1. Chromatic Intervals

Play in any combination. A suggested progression is:
- *Line A alone with recorded drone.* • *Line B alone with recorded drone.*
- *Line A and B combined with drone.* • *A, B and C combined (with and without recorded drone).*

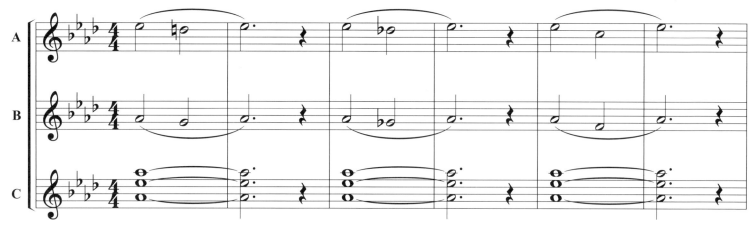

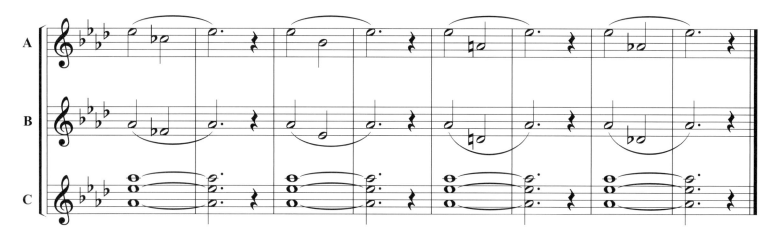

2. Interval Tuning

Play with recorded drone, then without.

3. Isolating Concert A♭

Play with recorded drone, then without.

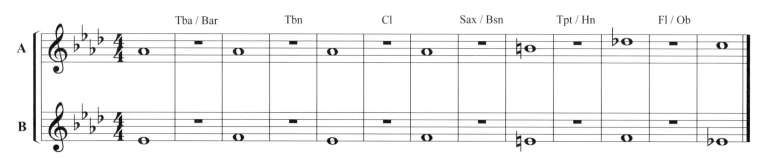

4. Chorale

Play using the following combinations:
- *With recorded drone.*
- *Without recorded drone, having various band members droning on concert A♭ and E♭.*
- *Chorale alone (without any drone).*

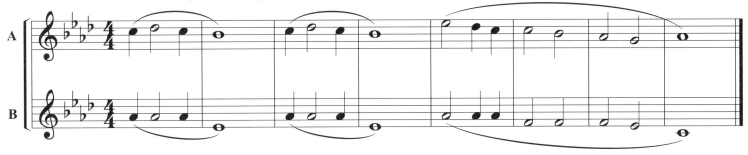

5. Concert F Minor Drone

Play with recorded drone, then without.

6. Descending Triads

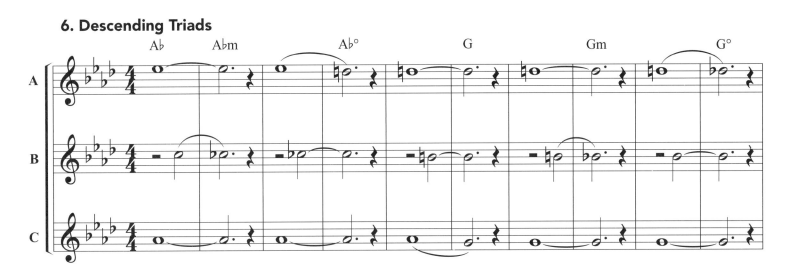

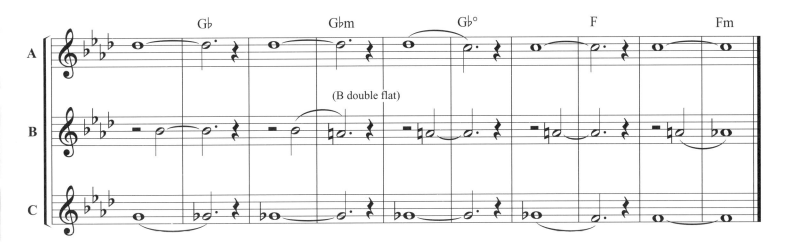

BB212PER

MAJOR AND MINOR SCALES

Play all scales with and without recorded drone. Suggested drone pitches are included for each scale.

Concert B♭ Major

Concert B♭ Minor

Concert E♭ Major

Concert E♭ Minor

Concert F Major

Concert F Minor

Concert C Major

Concert C Minor

Concert G Major

Concert G Minor

Concert D Major

Concert D Minor

Concert A Major

Concert A Minor

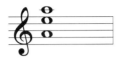

Concert E Major

Concert E Minor

Concert B Major

Concert B Minor

Concert G♭ Major

Concert G♭ (Concert F♯) Minor

Concert D♭ Major

Concert D♭ (Concert C♯) Minor

Concert A♭ Major

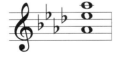

Concert A♭ Minor

12 CHORALES FOR BAND

BRIAN BALMAGES

Chorale No. 1 in B♭ Major

Chorale No. 2 in B♭ Major

Chorale No. 3 in G Minor

Chorale No. 4 in E♭ Major

Chorale No. 5 in E♭ Major

Chorale No. 6 in C Minor

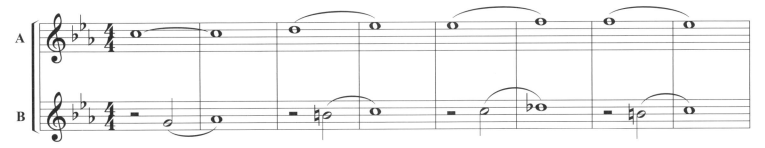

Chorale No. 7 in F Major

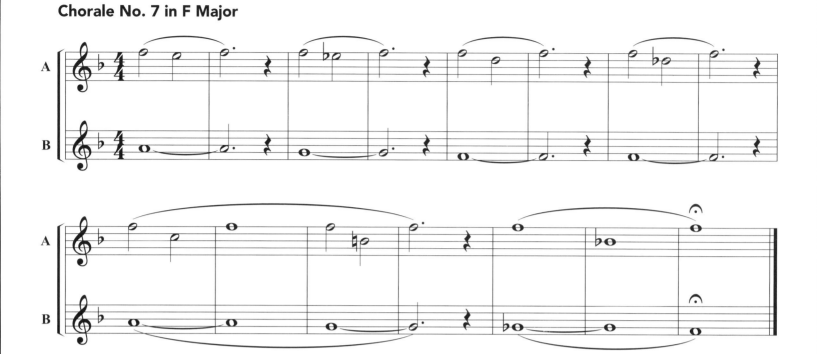

Chorale No. 8 in F Major

Chorale No. 9 in D Minor

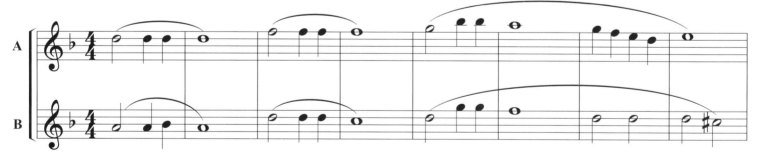

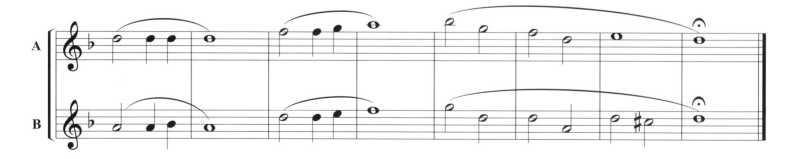

Chorale No. 10 in A♭ Major

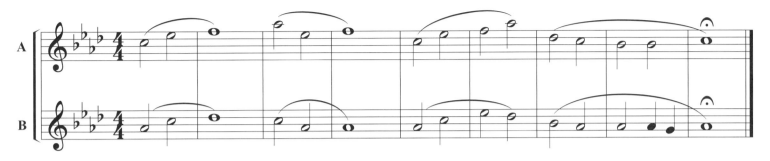

Chorale No. 11 in C Major

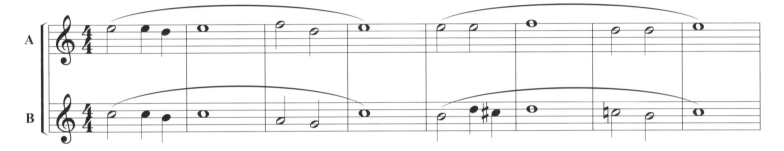

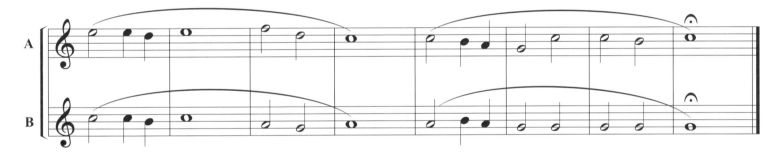

Chorale No. 12 in A Minor

WHOLE INSTRUMENT TUNING CHORALES

Full Band Comprehensive Tuning Chorale

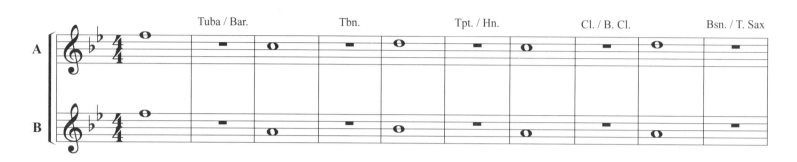

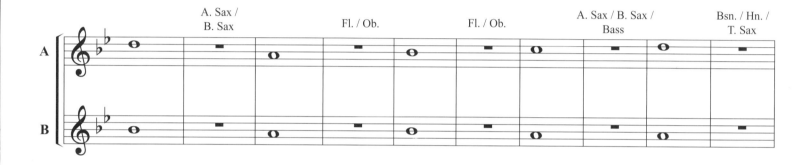

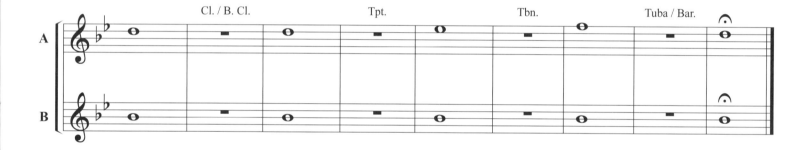